DEAR SANTA

ALL ISH I WANT
FOR CHRISTMAS
ISH FOR ALL MY
LOVED ONES
TO BE HAPPY

LOTS OF LOVE
SAMMY XXX

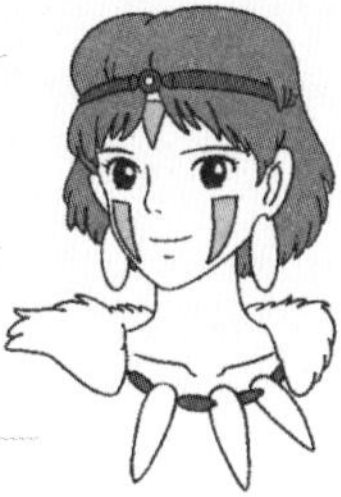

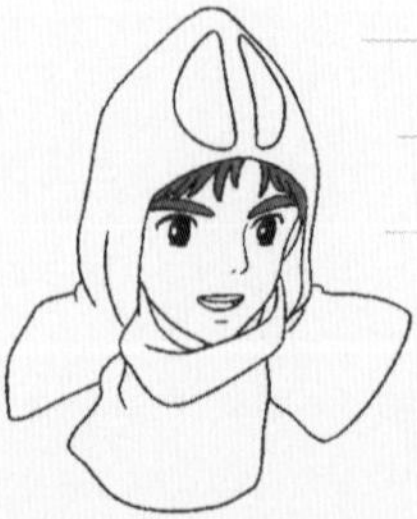

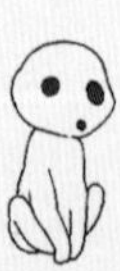

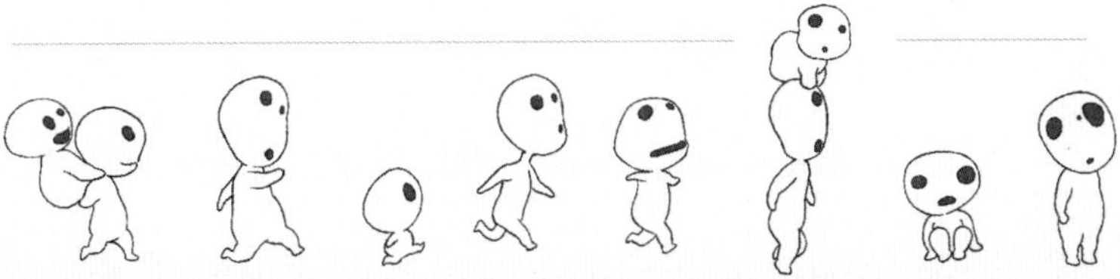

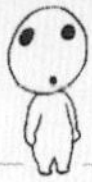
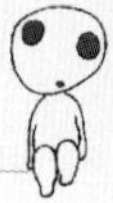
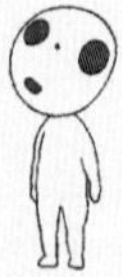
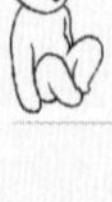

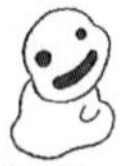

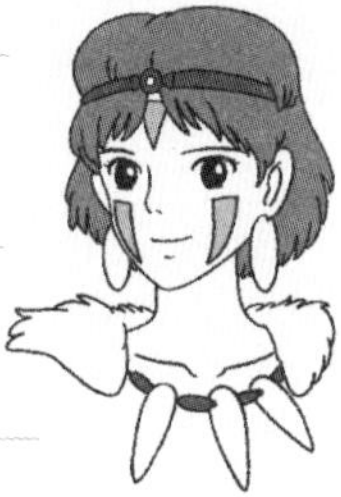

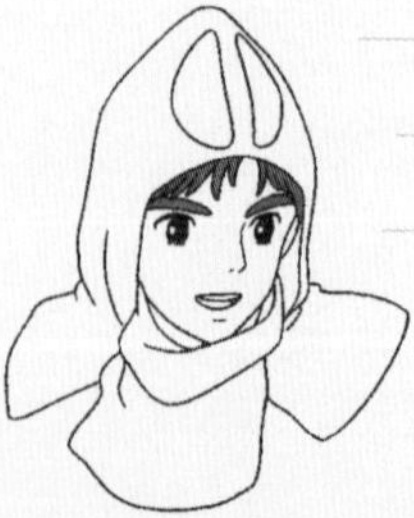

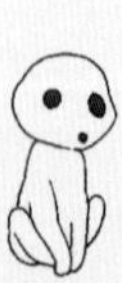

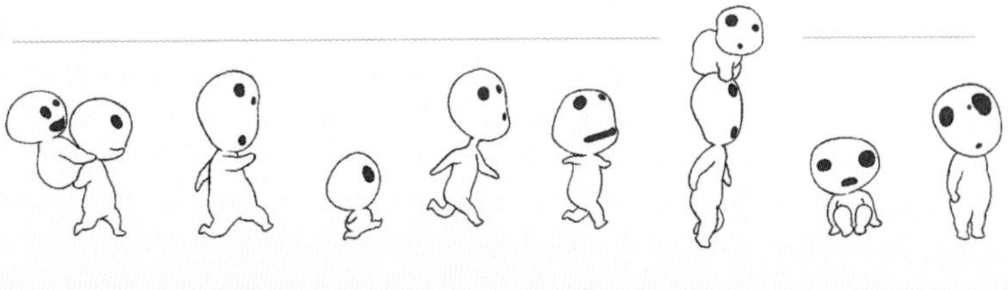

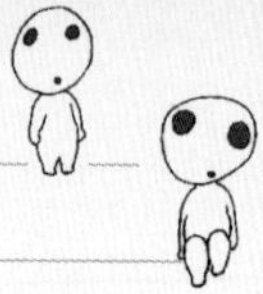
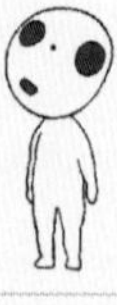
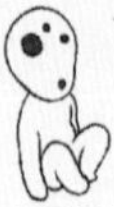

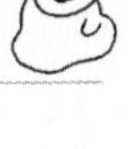

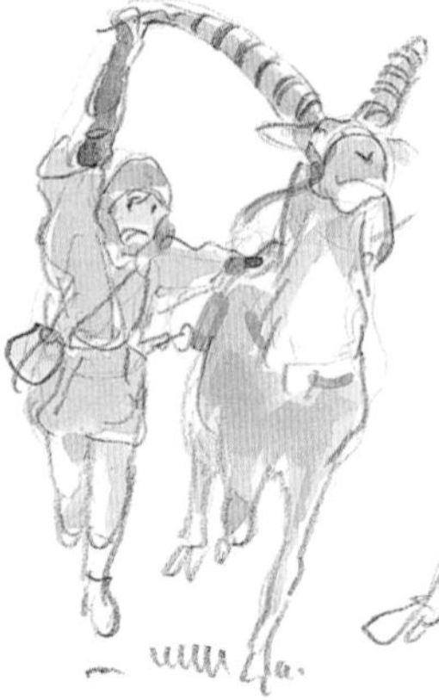

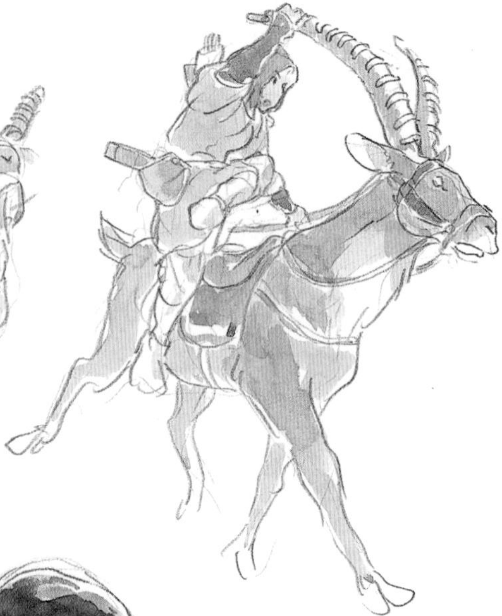

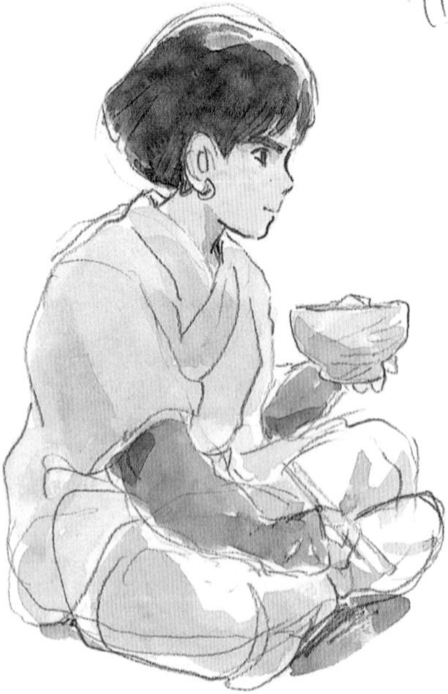

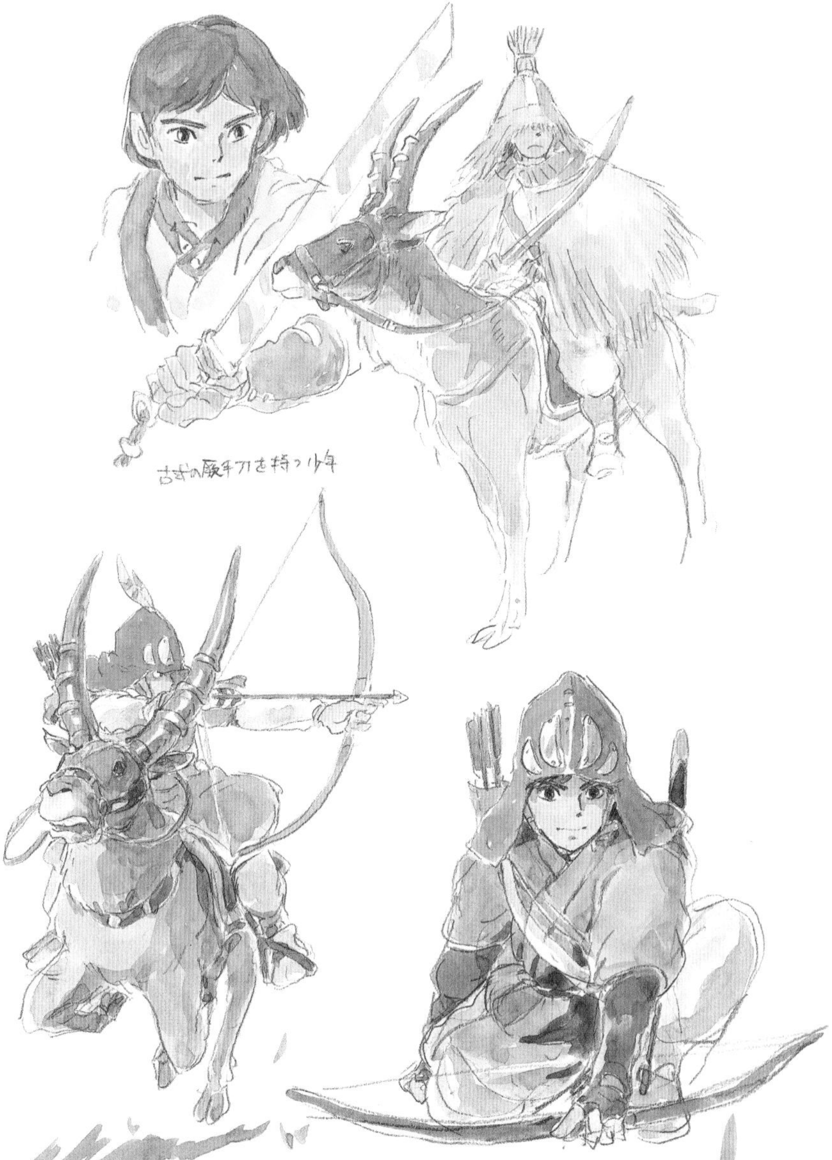
古式の蕨手刀を持つ少年

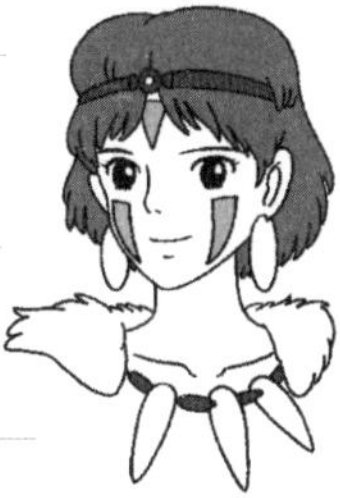

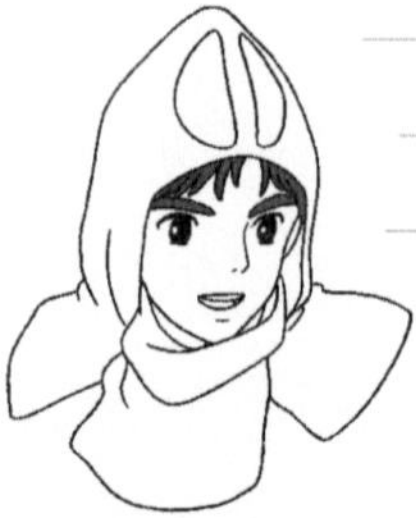

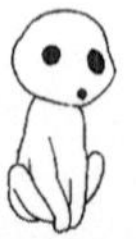

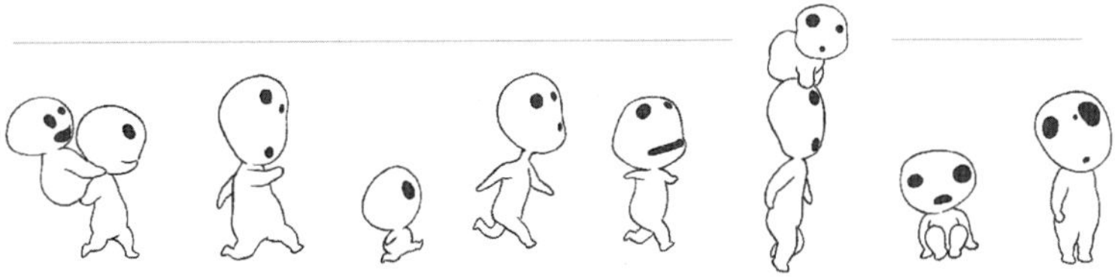

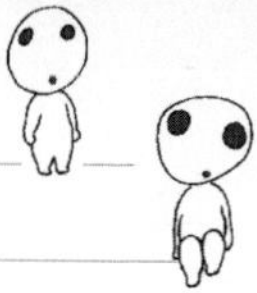

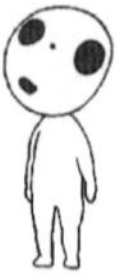

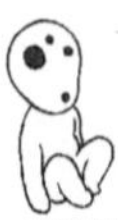

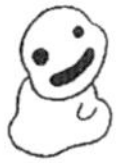

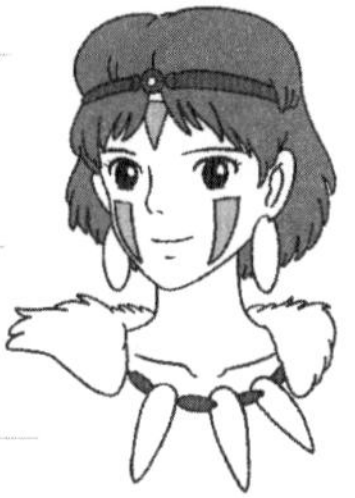

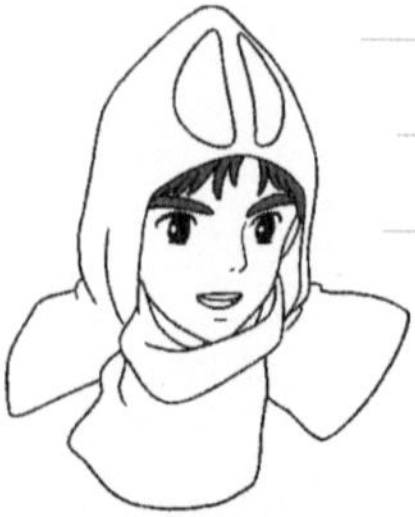

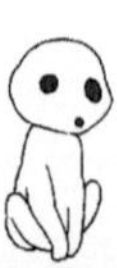

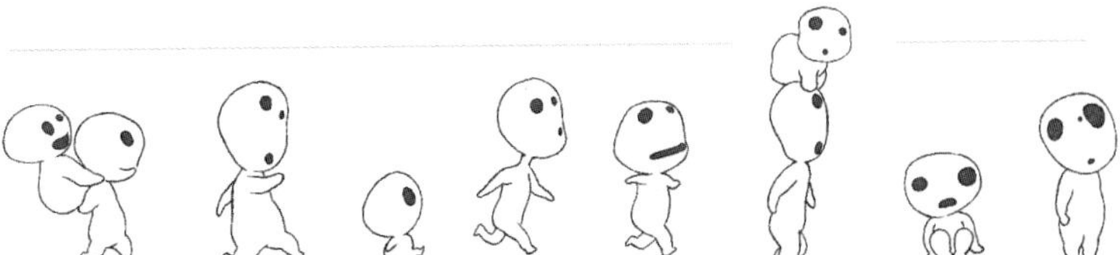

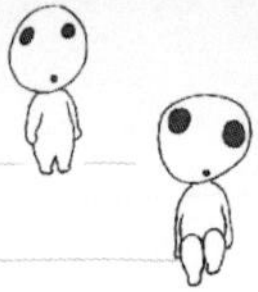

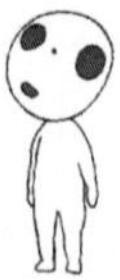

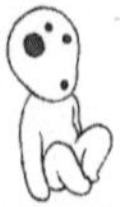

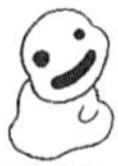

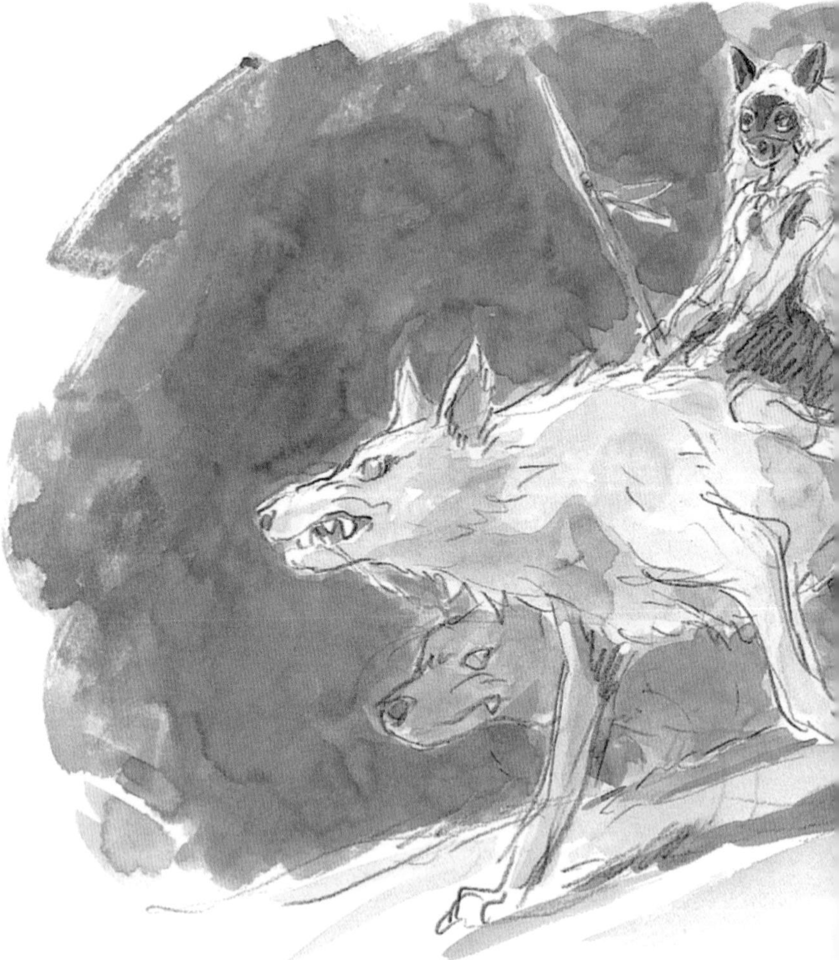

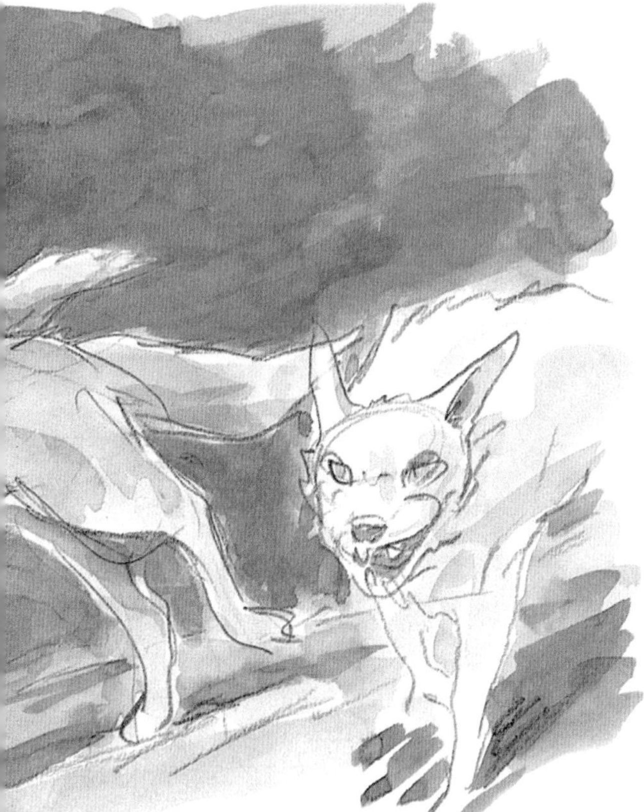

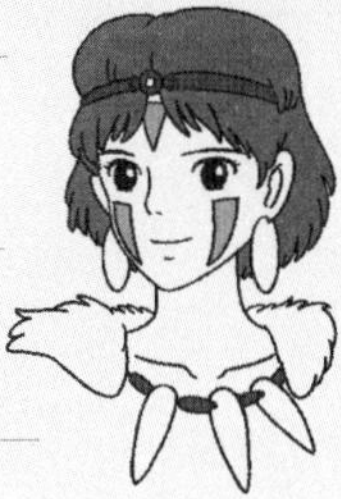

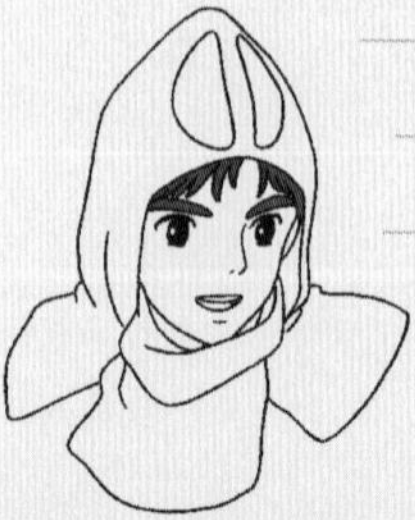

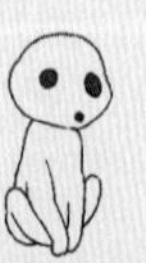

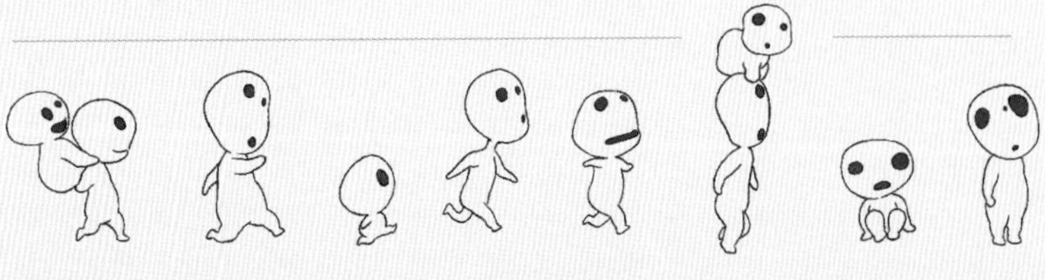

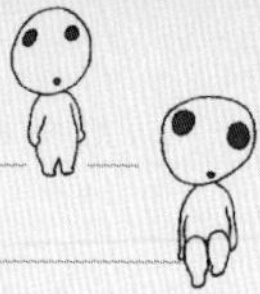

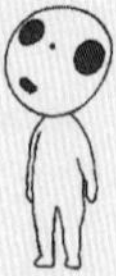

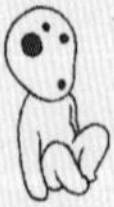

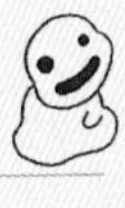

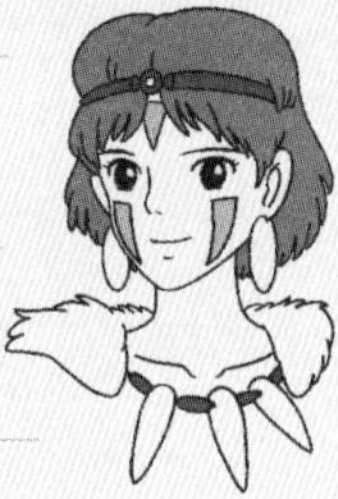

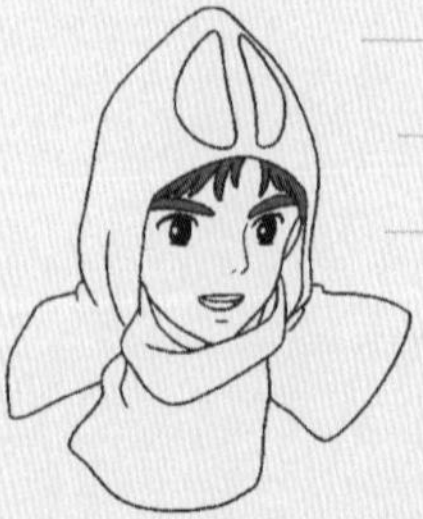

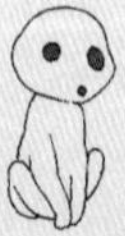

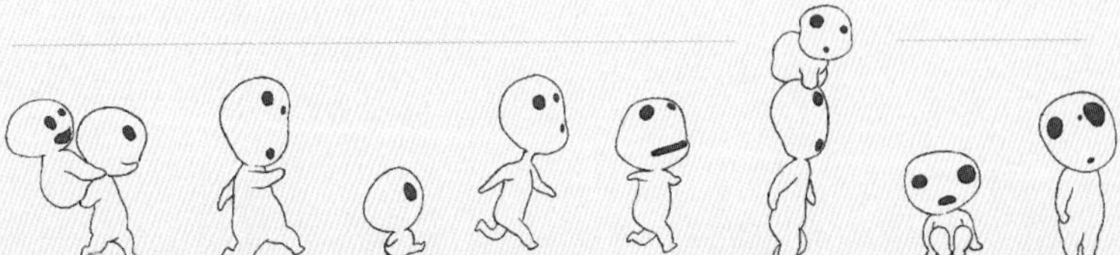

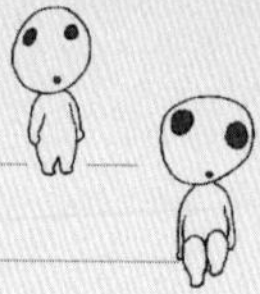

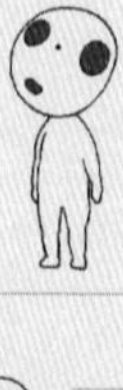

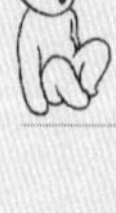

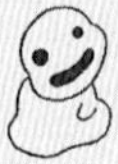

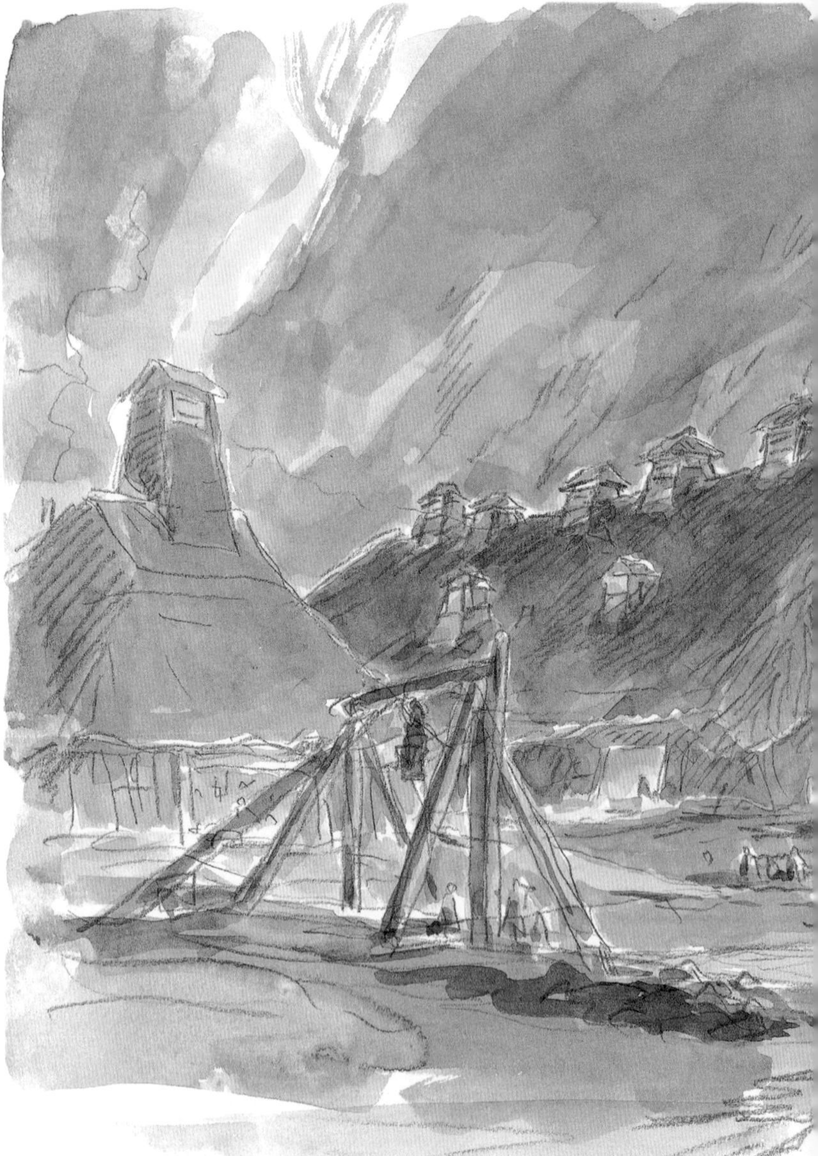

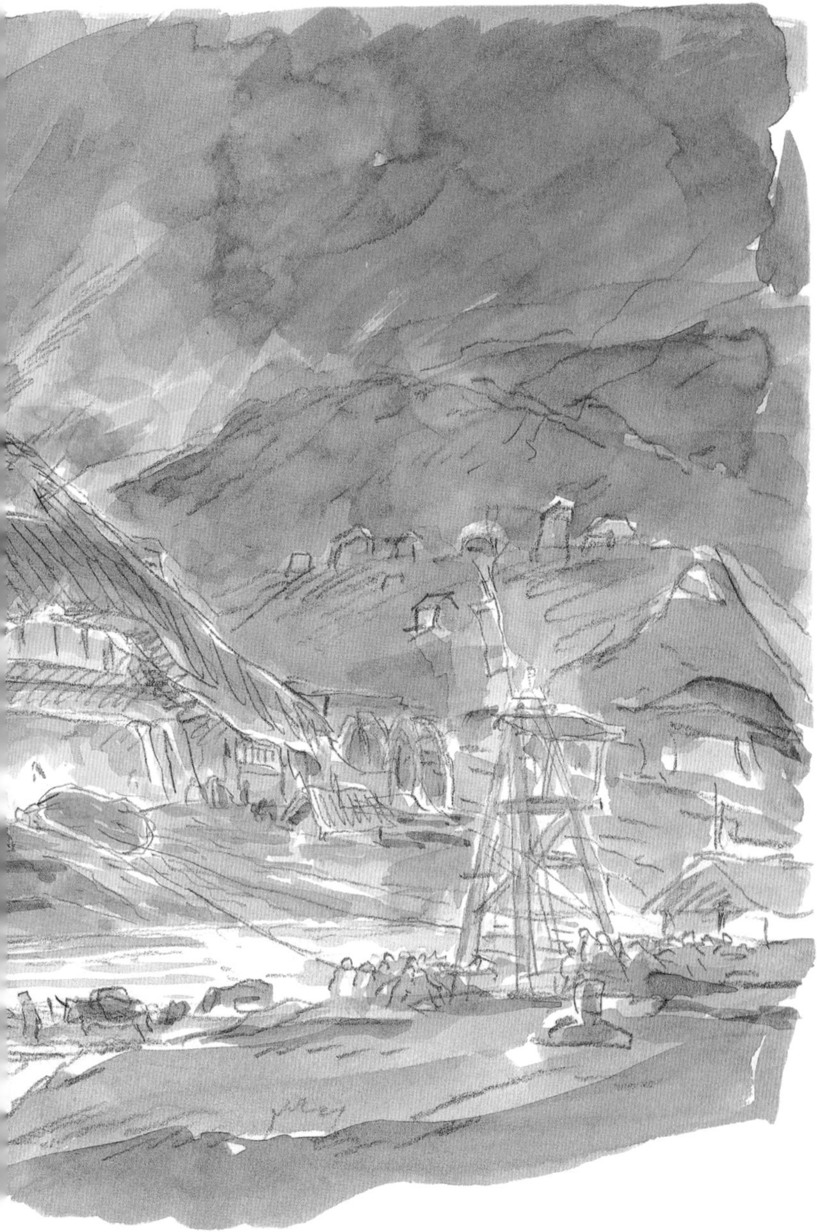

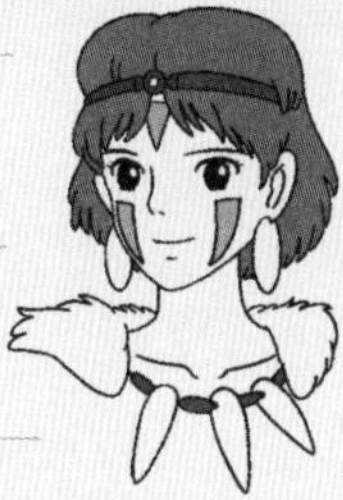

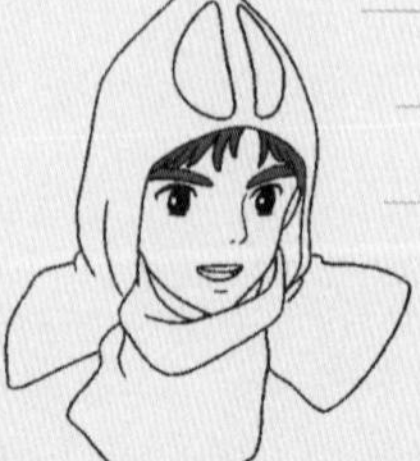

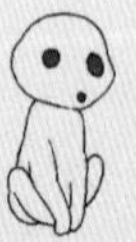

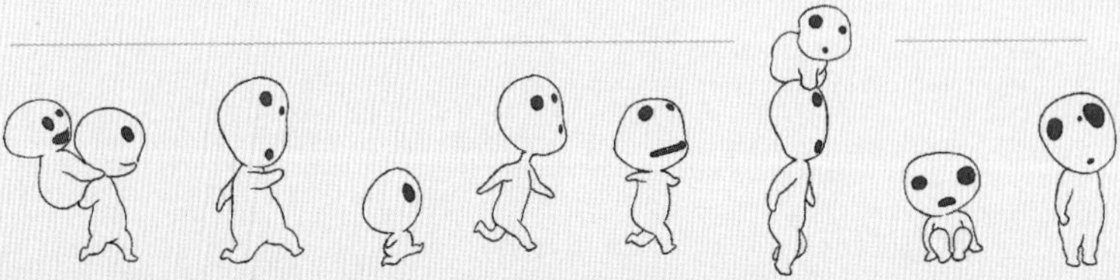

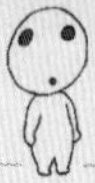
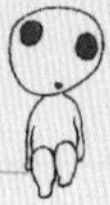
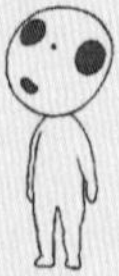
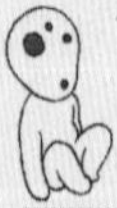

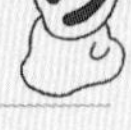

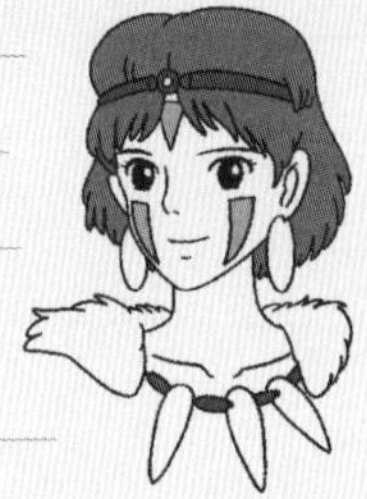

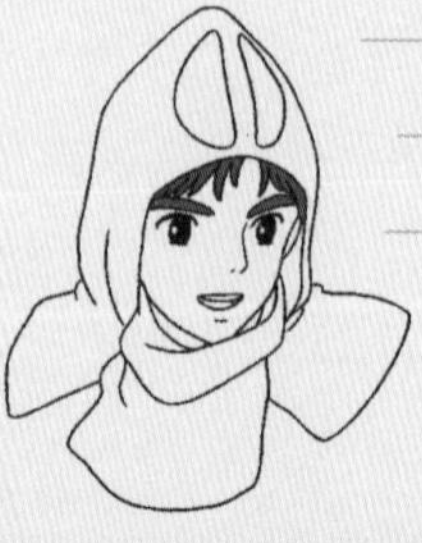

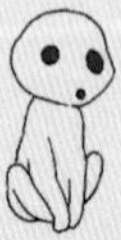

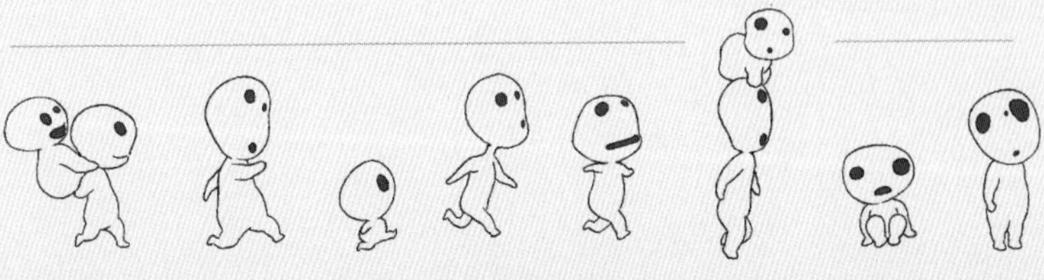

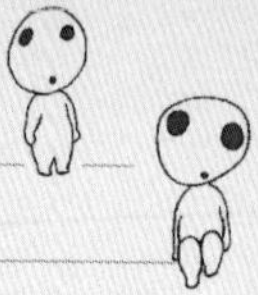

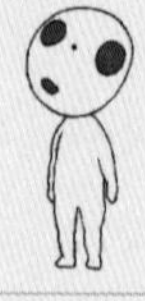

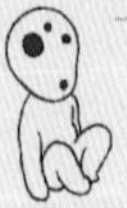

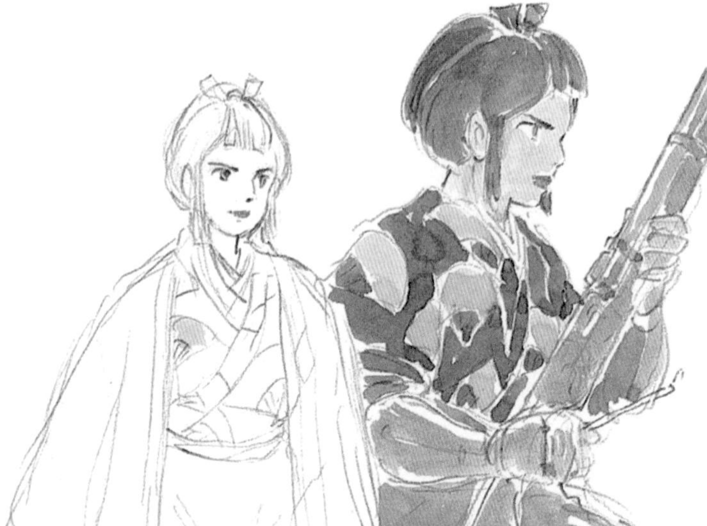

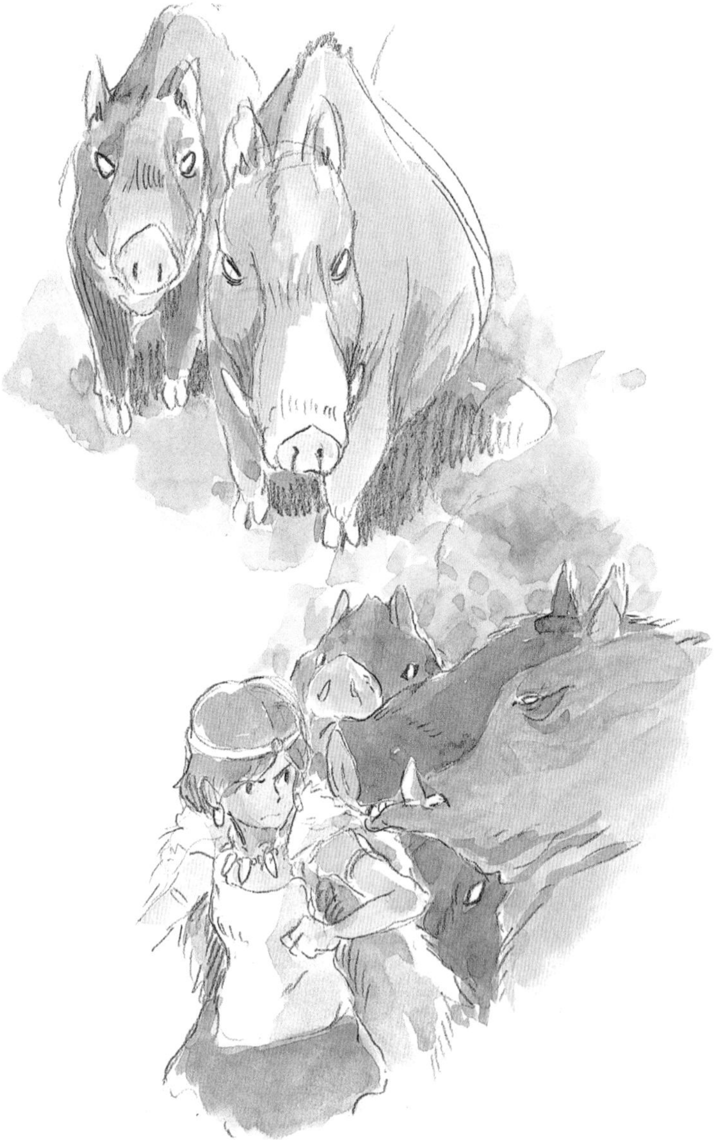

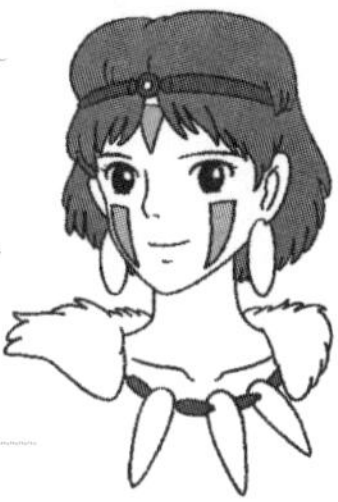

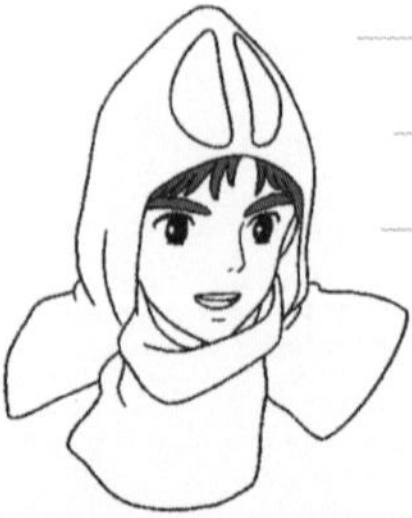

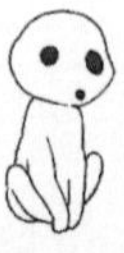

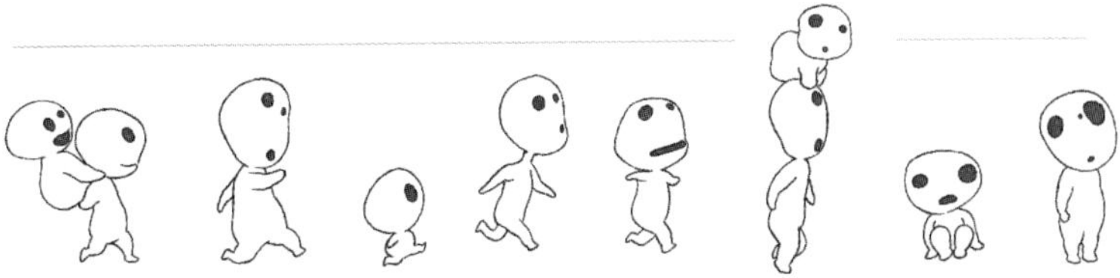

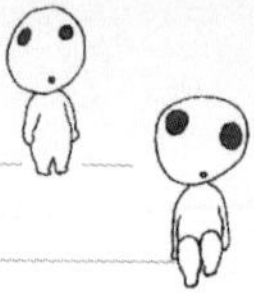

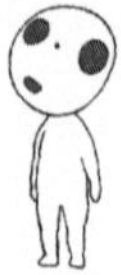

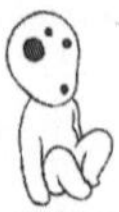

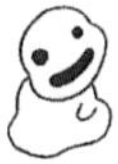

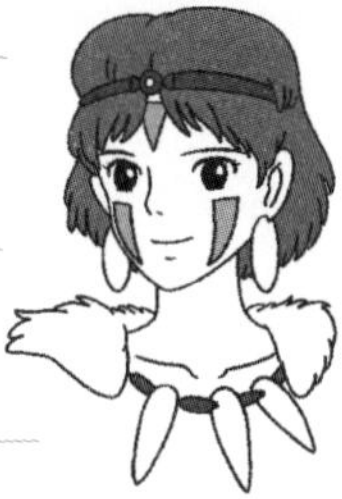

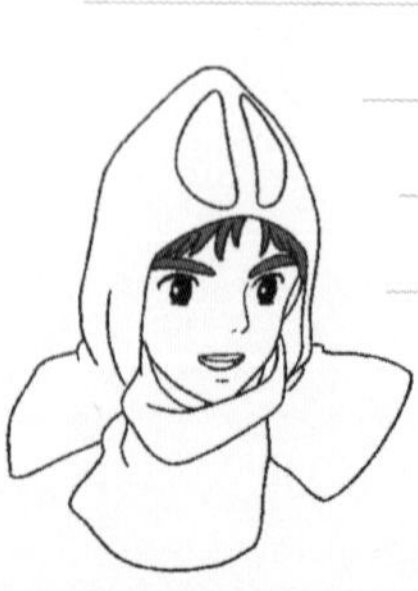

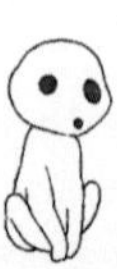

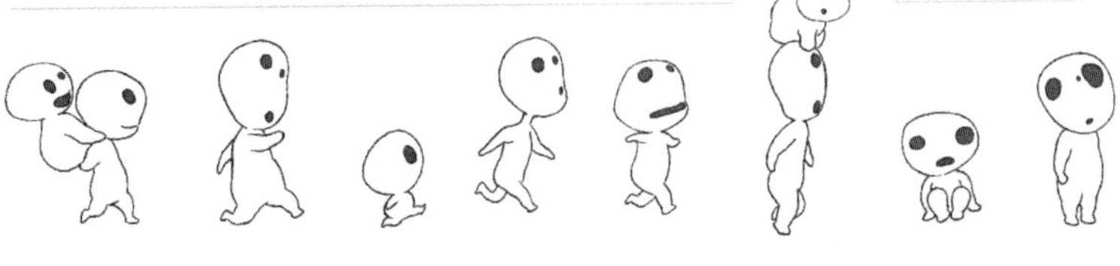

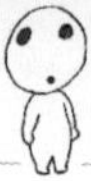
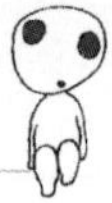
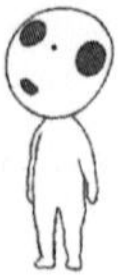
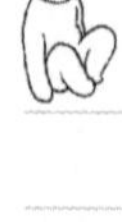

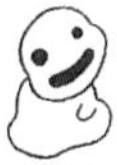

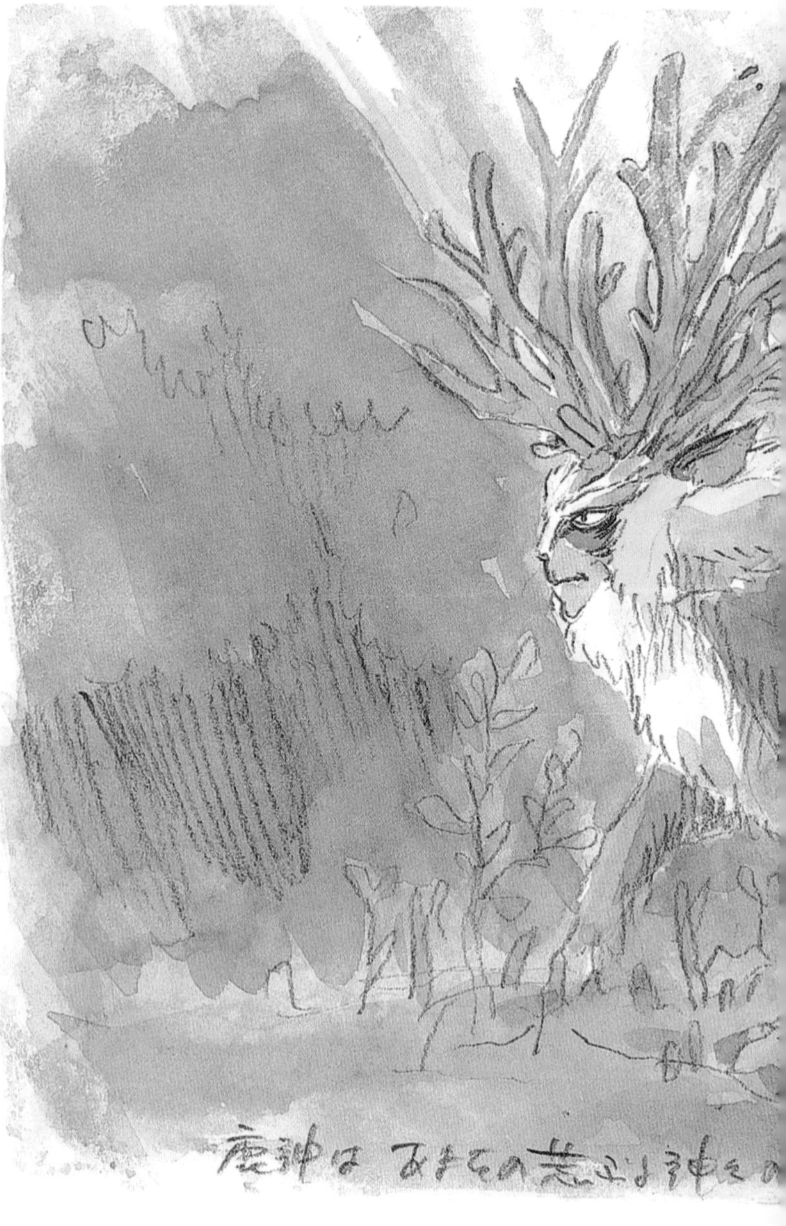
鹿神は あまたの荒ぶる神々の

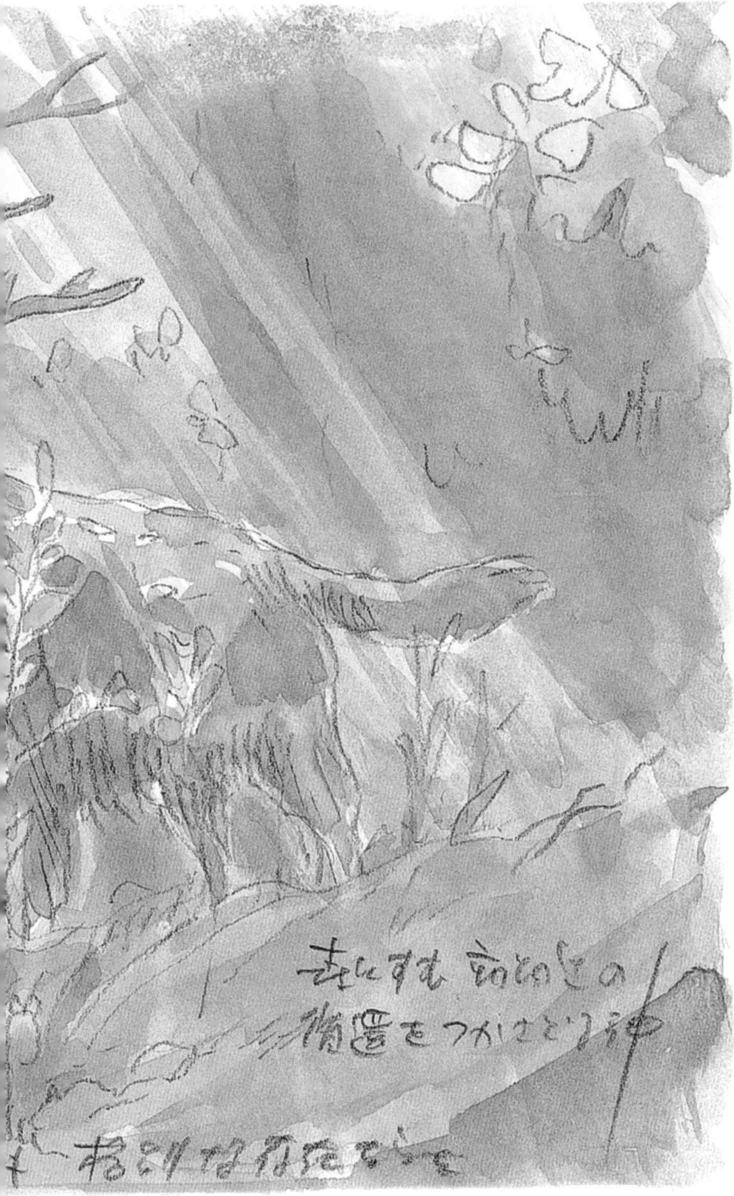
森にすむ動物との
循環をつかさどる神

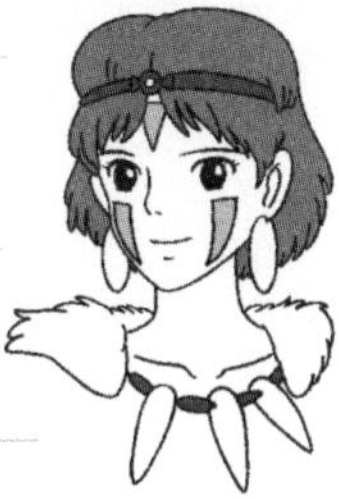

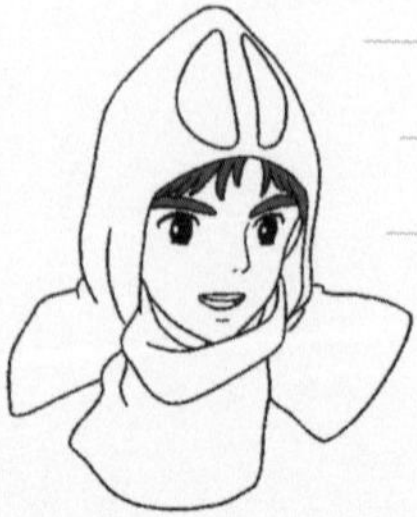

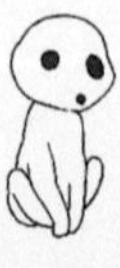

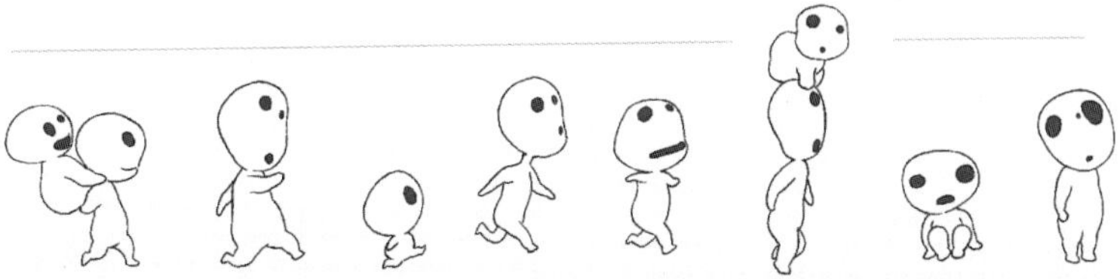

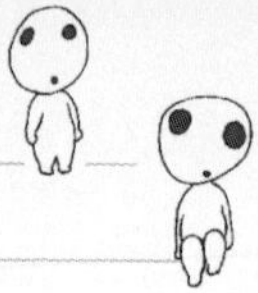

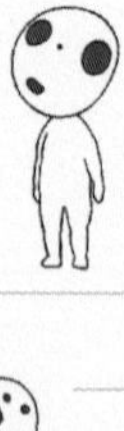

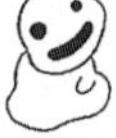

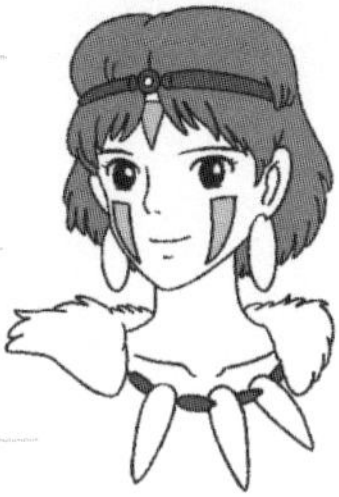